DOSTOEVSKY & GOGOL

TEXTS AND CRITICISM

Edited by

PRISCILLA MEYER
&
STEPHEN RUDY

ARDIS / / / ANN ARBOR

Dostoevsky and Gogol: Texts and Criticism

Edited and translated by Priscilla Meyer
and Stephen Rudy

Introduction by Priscilla Meyer and Stephen Rudy

Copyright©1979 by Ardis.

Published by Ardis,
2901 Heatherway,
Ann Arbor, Michigan 48104.

Manufactured in the United States of America.

ISBN 0-88233-315-1

Library of Congress Catalog Card No.: 79-51642

ACKNOWLEDGEMENTS

Grateful acknowledgement is made to the following for permission to quote from copyright material:

Fyodor Dostoevsky: "Uncle's Dream." Excerpts reprinted from *An Honest Thief and Other Stories*, translated by Constance Garnett, by permission of Macmillan Publishing Co., Inc., New York. Copyright ©1916 by Macmillan.

Fyodor Dostoevsky: *The Idiot.* Excerpts reprinted from *The Idiot*, translated by David Magarshack, by permission of Penguin Books Ltd., London. Copyright © 1955 by David Magarshack.

Fyodor Dostoevsky, *Netochka Nezvanova.* Excerpts reprinted from *Netochka Nezvanova,* translated by Ann Dunnigan, by permission of Prentice-Hall, Inc., Englewood Cliffs, New Jersey. Copyright © 1970 by Ann Dunnigan.

Boris Eikhenbaum: "How Gogol's 'Overcoat' is Made." Reprinted from "The Structure of Gogol's 'The Overcoat,'" translated by Beth Paul and Muriel Nesbitt, by permission of *The Russian Review*, Stanford, California. Copyright © 1963 by *The Russian Review*.

Nikolai Gogol: *The Collected Tales and Plays of Nikolai Gogol.* Excerpts reprinted from the *Collected Tales and Plays of Nikolai Gogol*, translated by Constance Garnett and Leonard Kent, by permission of Random House, Inc., New York. Copyright © 1964 by Random House.

Nikolai Gogol: *Dead Souls.* Excerpts reprinted from *Dead Souls*, translated by B.G. Guerney, by permission of Holt, Rinehart and Winston, Inc., New York. Copyright © 1942 by The Reader's Club.

Mikhail Bakhtin: "Discourse Typology in Prose." Excerpts reprinted from *Readings in Russian Poetics*, edited by L. Matejka and K. Pomorska, by permission of M.I.T. Press, Cambridge, Mass. Copyright © 1971 by M.I.T.

Gogol: *Selected Passages from a Correspondence with Friends.* Excerpts reprinted from *Selected Passages from a Correspondence with Friends*, translated by Jesse Zeldin, by permission of Vanderbilt University Press, Nashville, Tennessee. Copyright © 1969 by Vanderbilt University Press.

Thomas Mann, *Doctor Faustus.* Excerpts reprinted from *Doctor Faustus,* translated by H.T. Lowe-Porter, by permission of A.A. Knopf, New York. Copyright © 1948 by A.A. Knopf.

CONTENTS

PREFACE

This collection provides materials for understanding how Dostoevsky began his career as a writer by confronting Gogol's literary heritage. The topic is one that has occupied a central place in Russian literary criticism during the last century and served as the impetus for some of the most outstanding works of Formalist, as well as of more traditional, literary scholarship. Our purpose in translating the criticism included here is to make available to the English-speaking reader the best of the factually and methodologically rich heritage of Russian criticism on this topic.

Dostoevsky's early works (from the publication of *Poor Folk* in 1846 to his exile to Siberia in 1849) provide an exemplary model for a discussion of literary evolution in the context of a crucial period in Russian literature. In order to understand Dostoevsky's work fully, both close readings of the texts and the study of Russian literary evolution from the 1820s to the 1840s are essential. Neither has been possible in English criticism because of the absence of accurate translations of both Gogol and Dostoevsky and the ignorance of the Russian literary tradition, a situation which this collection, we hope, will amend.

We pay particular attention to the stories about the poor clerk, which respond to Gogol's later work, only alluding briefly in the foreword to the second stage of Dostoevsky's early period, which relates to Gogol's earlier writing. This anthology may be used as a companion to Dostoevsky's first two novels, *Poor Folk* and *The Double*. It is unfortunate that they are too long to be included here, because the existing translations do not convey the peculiarities of the heroes' speech, which is riddled with diminutives, folk sayings, and idiosyncratic juxtapositions of stylistic levels. We have translated quotations from these two novels ourselves, providing letter and chapter references respectively. For citations from other works we refer the reader to existing English translations, but in most cases we have substantially revised them. Hitherto the imprecision of the translations of the stories we include has made it impossible for the English reader to appreciate their style. We have made an effort to preserve Gogol's deliberate awkwardness of construction, his alliterations, redundancies and illogicalities, which are usually smoothed over or ignored. The same is true in our renderings of Dostoevsky's stories, especially where he imitates Gogol. This enables the reader to verify the stylistic analyses here given by consulting the English versions.

The texts we have used for Gogol's stories are those of the Academy of Sciences edition (1938) in which the parts originally censored, omitted in most translations, have been restored. The new Academy of Sciences edition (1971) of Dostoevsky's work is the source for "Mr. Prokharchin" and "Polzunkov." The translations of prose by Gogol and Dostoevsky are by Priscilla Meyer; the critical articles, unless otherwise specified, are translated by Stephen Rudy.

For a chronology of Gogol's work we refer the reader to *The Collected Tales of Nikolai Gogol*, edited by Leonard Kent. Konstantin Mochulsky's *Dostoevsky, His Life and Work* provides a complete biography and chronology.

In the body of the text the system of transliteration, with minor exceptions, is that used in D.S. Mirsky's *History of Russian Literature*, which the reader may wish to consult for general background information as well. In the scholarly apparatus we use a modified Library of Congress system. This makes pronunciation easier for non-Russian-speakers without sacrificing accuracy for those doing research in Russian.

We would like to thank Wesleyan University and the Ford Foundation for generous grants which made our work possible. We are grateful to the late Dmitry Chizhevsky for permission to include his article, and to Peter Stetson for his fine translation of Bem's article. Thanks are also due to Nancy Martin for typing the manuscript. We are particularly indebted to Greta Slobin, Michael Holquist, Vadim Liapunov, Krystyna Pomorska and Roman Jakobson for their invaluable aid and comments. Roger, Bill, Ilona and Krista provided crucial patience and support.

INTRODUCTION

I

Influence studies have been in ill repute among literary scholars for at least the last half century—and deservedly so. The dangers inherent in such an approach are reason enough for this fact. It is impossible in most cases to prove conclusively the existence of a given influence, inasmuch as external features of style and theme are most often the common property of an entire generation of writers and too easily deceive the overeager investigator into mistaking convergences or coincidences for the direct influence of one writer on another.[1] Furthermore, a given influence, even if firmly established by literary and extraliterary documentation, may prove quite irrelevant for the total scheme of a writer's work and merely add to the catalogue of disconnected literary facts. Finally, there are "deep psychological and personal influences which are not reflected on the literary level at all."[2] But beyond these inherent dangers, the distrust of this particular avenue of research reflects a larger shift in the methodology of literary studies that has rendered the question of influences as such a marginal or insignificant problem.

This shift in methodology owes much to the heritage of Russian Formalism. The early Formalists attempted to establish a concrete poetics that would investigate individual works with the aim of determining the specific, intrinsic characteristics of verbal art: the emphasis was on "art as device" and on how particular works are made. This immanent approach reflected their insistence on the autonomy of literary studies and their rejection of social criteria and psychologism in the analysis of literature. Eikhenbaum's study, "How Gogol's 'Overcoat' Is Made," is an exemplary work of early Formalism in this respect. Rejecting the prevalent "social" interpretation of Gogol's short story and in particular of its so-called "humane" passage, Eikhenbaum focuses on the narrative devices that determine the composition of "The Overcoat" and examines the function that the "humane" passage fulfilled within that overall compositional system. The conclusions he reaches about the grotesque nature of the story could be generalized to include the writer's entire work, a point that Slonimsky was later to make in examining *Gogol's Comic Technique*,[3] or be seen in terms of Gogol's evolution as a writer (which Vinogradov criticizes him for failing to do—see p. 181 below), but Eikhenbaum limits himself primarily to the material at hand. His primary interest is an exhaustive investigation of a specific text as it relates to one area of poetics, namely the theory of the grotesque.[4]

The "immanent" method was developed by the Formalists in their pursuit of the object of literary science, the object here being taken as the "literariness" of a work, its specifically literary devices. While this method was valid in its attempt at descriptive adequacy and its avoidance of the value judgments that characterize traditional literary criticism, it was inadequate because of the splendid isolation it imposed on literary works, not only from the social and cultural context, but even from the context of literary history. Tynyanov, who grasped the historical nature of "literariness," asked: "Is the so-called 'immanent' study of a work as a system possible outside its correlation with the system of literature?"[5] He concluded that it was impossible, even in respect to contemporary literature. Even if individual works were understood not merely as sum totals of their devices but as systems, i.e. functional interdependencies of elements hierarchically ordered and with a "dominant," the dynamic and functional nature of literature as a whole could not be appreciated:

> It is exclusively in terms of its evolution that we shall be able to arrive at an analytical "definition" of literature. . . . Literature . . . is a dynamic verbal construction. The requirement of incessant dynamism is what brings evolution about, seeing that every dynamic system necessarily becomes automatized and a constructional principle of an opposite kind dialectically comes into play.[6]

Evolution was to become the primary factor in understanding literary processes that had previously been examined, more often than not statically, under the rubric of "influences."[7]

This concern with the dynamism of literary works underlies Tynyanov's essay on "Dostoevsky and Gogol." His primary concern is to demonstrate that Gogol's influence on Dostoevsky is a much more complicated problem than literary historians, content with tracing motifs or stylistic features, would have us believe. The question is not simply the circle of devices that Dostoevsky "borrowed" from Gogol, but what use he put them to and what his very selection can tell us about his work. Tynyanov circumscribes the problem of influence by pointing out the larger theoretical issue that subsumes it, namely the problem of literary polemics. Literary works do not exist in a vacuum; they are dynamic works which respond to the literary system preceding them. Tynyanov proposes two theoretical factors to use in analyzing what an author does with the devices he borrows from his predecessors: stylization and parody. The latter notion, which Tynyanov understands in its broad sense, is a fundamental characteristic of almost any literary work that challenges a given tradition. In the case of Dostoevsky it proves to be the determining characteristic of his early work.

The emphasis in later Formalism on the "evolutionary" dynamism underlying the structure of literary works and on their functional significance is apparent throughout Viktor Vinogradov's *The Evolution of Russian Naturalism* and particularly in the essay translated here, "The School of Sentimental Naturalism (Dostoevsky's *Poor Folk* against the Background of the Literary Evolution of the 1840s)." Vinogradov approaches Dostoevsky's first novel from two points of view which he labels the "functional, immanent" and the "retrospective, projective" approaches.[8] The first examines the work as a "self-contained system of stylistic interrelations, the functional basis of which is the immanent goal realized in the creation of the work"; the second "sketches the structuration of an artistic work against the background of chronologically contiguous, homogeneous literary structures, as the realization of a new synthesis of the forms presented in them and, consequently, as their transformation, or as an act of destroying the ruling styles by reviving and creatively regenerating outlived forms." Vinogradov finds the first method indispensable for the construction of a comprehensive "literary theory" or poetics, the second for a "literary history," but, as he stresses, the two approaches are "mutually interdependent and inseparable."

Vinogradov pays a great deal of attention to the "secondary" writers of the period in an attempt to elucidate the common "language of literature"[9] confronted by Dostoevsky at the beginning of his career. He makes a particular point of emphasizing that the devices and even the combinations of devices used by Dostoevsky that are often cited as the direct "influence" of Gogol are "collective—like the grammatical categories of a language; they are the accomplishment of a literary school."[10] Gogol's own work was misread by his contemporaries, who saw it only in the perspective of the school which it was thought to represent and therefore failed to discern its true evolutionary pattern. Vinogradov goes so far as to assert that "influence has no place" in a history of literature that is concerned with the "evolution of literary systems," since each system contains "in microcosm . . . the reflection of the forms of previous literary traditions and the potential tendencies of future transformations" into new systems. Devices which might be taken as influences because of external similarities "turn out to be internally motivated by the immanent evolution of the system," and "the principle of influence is superfluous for an historical elucidation" of these devices. As Victor Erlich has stated in his study of the Formalists' concern with "literary dynamics," the Formalists discovered that the essential thing in questions of influence was often "not what the 'lender' does best, but what the 'borrower' needs most."[11] Vinogradov's study is a fine analysis of how the system of a literary work fits into the system of literature of its time and exemplifies the type of literary history that the Formalists attempted to construct, one that would not simply "review a chaos of manifold phenomena and orders of phenomena."[12]

The final stage of Formalist literary theory was concerned with the problem of relating purely literary systems to social, psychological and cultural systems. The so-called "Bakhtin School," a group of scholars who tried to integrate Formalist methods with Marxist criticism, laid the groundwork for a solution of this problem.[13] They attempted to construct a general theory of discourse that could show how the various functions of language operate vis-à-vis the roles of "author," "reader," and "hero" in structuring the "ideology" (that is, the system of value judgments) of a literary work. Bakhtin's essay included here is from his book *Problems of Dostoevsky's Poetics* (first edition 1929), in which Bakhtin elaborated such a typology of discourse and applied it to Dostoevsky's works. The particular section deals with Dostoevsky's first two novels, *Poor Folk* and *The Double*, and it is interesting to see how Bakhtin extends the analyses of literary functions made by Tynyanov and Vinogradov within the wider framework of the social and psychological functions implicit in a work of literature. Bakhtin's book is one of the best pieces written about Dostoevsky, both from a critical and theoretical standpoint.

The one genuine "influence study" included here is by A.L. Bem, a sensitive literary critic who was not content with mere "juxtapositions" of themes and stylistically coincident passages. Bem examines the function of Gogol's "The Nose" as a subtext for Dostoevsky's *The Double*, using the method of "close reading." The fact of influence here is placed within the larger framework of Dostoevsky's polemic with Gogol, the theoretical basis for which was provided by the studies of Tynyanov and Bakhtin contained in this volume.

II

The early 1830s marked a crucial turning point in the history of Russian literature. Poetry, which had its "Golden Age" in the first quarter of the century, was giving way to prose. This shift can be at least partly explained by the fact that verse had been cultivated to such a point of excellence that even the mediocre poetry of the late 1820s was being written in a well-formed poetic language (in terms of vocabulary, syntax, meter, genres, etc.). Prose, on the other hand, was in a chaotic state and completely lacked norms of style and genre. It was split between two unreconciled poles: that of antiquated bookish language, which, despite Karamzin's reforms, basically dated to the XVIIIth century and was suitable only for "lofty" topics; and that of conversational speech, too crude to be used as a basis of the literary language. The crucial task of the literature of the time was to establish a prose language that could bridge the gap between the "high" and "low" level of Russian and serve as a basis for elaborating a range of genres and normative styles.[14]

The experiments of the late 1820s and the early 1830s in Russian prose ran the gamut from writing influenced by foreign models, especially in terms of syntax, to the stylized and folksy language of Dahl's fairytales[15] or the historical novels of the time. The latter, a return to Old Russian, was clearly impossible ("We should learn to speak in Russian and not just in fairytales," as Pushkin said).[16] By the beginning of the 1830s two types of prose had emerged: one which opposed itself to poetry by its simplicity and exactness of expression (best exemplified by the prose of the poet Pushkin); the other, "ornamental" prose that was oriented on verse, using rhythmic and declamatory patterns of speech. Boris Eikhenbaum puts it as follows: "As in France the line extending from Chateaubriand to Hugo is opposed to that extending from Mérimée to Stendhal, so in Russia the prose of Marlinsky and Gogol, in part going back to the prose of Karamzin . . . is opposed to that of Pushkin."[17] "Ornamental" prose had the more immediate impact, since it permitted a greater range of styles.[18]

This opposition is strikingly illustrated by the appearance in 1831, a few months apart, of Pushkin's *Tales of Belkin* and Gogol's *Evenings on a Farm Near Dikanka*. Both were short-story cycles using the "frame" device, most likely derived from Walter Scott's "Tales of My Landlord,"[19] of having a fictitious "publisher or editor" introduce a group of stories written down by a central narrator and gathered from various "storytellers."

While Pushkin used anecdotal plots and concentrated on normalizing the prose style of his narrator, Gogol played the role of a "Russian Walter Scott" and submerged his readers in the "ethnography" of the Ukraine. His "Ukraine" was an amalgam of folklore and local legend and the German *Kunstmärchen* tradition,[20] with stereotyped figures from the Ukrainian puppet-theatre *(vertep)* acting out mechanical love intrigues, the interest of which was not in the situation but in the *telling*. The latter fact causes the comic side of the diabolic and fantastic to far outweigh their tragic side, as the concern with narrative devices and absurdities of everyday, vulgar language dominate every aspect of these tales.

Gogol's primary device in the *Evenings* was the *skaz*, narration presented by a narrator distinct from the author and endowed with a verbal manner characterizing his personality and social milieu.[21] The formal features of this type of narration are amply demonstrated by "The Tale of Captain Kopeykin" from Gogol's *Dead Souls* (1842), parts of which are quoted by Chizhevsky in his discussion of "The Overcoat" (see below, p. 142). In *Evenings* the comic effects of the *skaz* are as much a product of the context as of its formal characteristics. The narrator presents his story to a set of listeners who are part of a close circle of acquaintances. Many of his asides are elliptical, taking for granted his audience's comprehension, or, on the contrary, are elaborate and amplify details that would be of interest *only* to that audience. Yet the story is being read by a reader foreign to that circle, thus creating a comic disparity between the events of the "little" world of the provincial storyteller and their lack of significance in terms of the "greater" world of the educated reader. This is the germ of the grotesque as it will appear eleven years later in Gogol's "The Overcoat": "The situation or event described [is] contained in a world, small to the point of the fantastic, of artificial experiences . . . completely cut off from the larger reality" (Eikhenbaum, p. 132 below; cf. Chizhevsky on the same point, p. 150 below). This disparity between two sets of perceptions, the reader's and the narrator's, gives the author full scope to play with the larger disharmony between things as they exist and as they are spoken about. The anomalies of language, the seemingly innocent slips and mannerisms of the "storyteller's" speech, his play with words, mask the author's more purposeful and often more sinister play with the world.

In *Evenings* the *skaz* is motivated characterologically. The "publisher," Rudy Panko the Beekeeper, introduces his narrators with characterizations that serve to justify the varieties and types of style employed in the tales. Yet Gogol's *skaz* often sparkles with a display of verbal fireworks that cannot possibly be subsumed under the image of any one narrator: the author shows his hand. One finds in *Evenings* the two styles that are the earmark of Gogol's entire creative output. Vasily Rozanov was the first to isolate and describe these styles: "The features of the one rise infinitely upward, those of the other [descend] downward"—an opposition of "endless *lyricism*" and the "dead fabric" of naturalistic "waxen language."[22] In *Evenings* the "endless lyricism" is most apparent in the nature descriptions (as it will be in all of Gogol's works from the first volume of *Evenings* to the second volume of *Dead Souls*), which are based on the metaphorical rhetoric of late romanticism, with a particularly sentimental, idealistic tinge. This lyricism is also present in Gogol's imitations of the style of folk poetry, which have more in common with rhetorical, ornamental prose than they have with the folk tradition. One contemporary critic, Polevoy, labelled this element of Gogol's style "soaringly incomprehensible flights" of words. The other element, which has been characterized as Gogol's naturalistic style, is based on the rambling dialectal speech of his storytellers, whose inability to express themselves often borders on verbal pathology. In Gogol's mature style, naturalistic description is so extreme that it results in a confusion between people and things, between the animate and the inanimate. When Gogol transfers this latter style from the field of folklore plots to the novella-farce based on a grotesque anecdote, as in "The Tale of How Ivan Ivanovich Quarreled with Ivan Nikiforovich" (referred to henceforth as "The Two Ivans"), the first stylistic layer, that of "endless lyricism," is downgraded and deliberately misapplied. The narrator's style has by this point lost what little characterological motivation it had, and disintegrates into a succession of verbal masks. This hybrid of inverted naturalism and lyricism distorts the fictional universe, and this in turn casts doubt upon reality itself.

In *Mirgorod* (1835), Gogol turns to a variety of different genres in his effort to transcend the limitations placed on him by material from the Ukrainian milieu. Besides "The Two Ivans," the volume contains "Old World Landowners," in which Gogol parodies the ancient and still popular sentimental genre of the idyll by introducing comic and ironic motifs that undercut the "idyllic" life of the old couple who are its heroes. The denouement, death in the shape of a black cat summoning Pulkheria Ivanovna, illustrates "the tragedy of insignificant events," which had been treated on a more vulgar, comic level in "The Two Ivans." In "Viy," Gogol uses the folkloristic demonology of *Evenings*, but describes the terrifying visions of the seminarian at the end of the story in such detail that contemporary reviewers were offended. The rhetoric of the story clearly shows the influence of that late and short-lived branch of French romanticism called the "école frénétique"[23] (see Vinogradov, p. 162 ff. below). The same is present to a lesser degree in Gogol's historical novel, *Taras Bulba*, particularly in the depiction of tortures and executions.

In 1835 Gogol also published *Arabesques,* a collection of assorted "odds and ends," including essays on history and culture and earlier attempts at historical fiction in the mode of the *école frénétique*, as well as three of Gogol's best stories: "The Portrait," "Nevsky Prospect," and "The Diary of a Madman." "The Portrait," a variation on the romantic *Kunstnovel*, is the weakest of the three. It traces the rise and fall of an artist who has ruined his talent through ambition and by "selling out to the Devil," with a rather facile "prehistory" in the second part explaining the origin of the demonic force of the portrait and the fantastic events that have issued from it. The second of the group, "Nevsky Prospect," is a masterpiece in which Gogol successfully completes the transition from the Ukrainian milieu of his earlier works to the Petersburg setting in a synthesis of his two lines of attack on the poetics of romantic idealization: "High" genres are subtly overturned and "low" genres portray the seamy side of life in a farcical manner. The story is constructed on the basis of two contrasting parallel plots. The first traces the unfortunate "Petersburg artist" Piskaryov's pursuit of a "perfect Bianca of Perugino" whom he encounters on Nevsky Prospect and who turns out to be a common prostitute; he cannot bear the disillusionment and kills himself. Here the *Kunstnovel* of Hoffmann and German Romanticism is mingled with motifs from the urban novels of the *école frénétique* and the incidental motif of opium derived from De Quincey.[24] The other plot is the story of Lieutenant Pirogov, who is out for easier prey, but instead gets involved with the wife of a solid (and drunken) German workman. It is basically a reworking in a vaudeville vein of an officer's anecdote about an unsuccessful seduction, with one farcical scene which mocks the romantic sources of the first plot (the quarrel between the two German workmen named Schiller and Hoffmann). These two plots are framed by a description of Nevsky Prospect inspired by the journalistic feuilleton then in vogue.[25] (This genre, which became popular when the *école frénétique* shifted from historical to urban settings, was the germ of the Russian "physiological sketch" that was to become the standard genre of the Natural School—cf. Vinogradov, p. 166 ff. below.) In "Nevsky Prospect," Gogol reworks all three of these traditions—the romantic *Kunstnovel,* the urban novel of the *école frénétique*, and the journalistic feuilleton—and unifies them by the pervasive motif of delusion. The numerous demonic figures of the Ukraine have been transformed into the unobtrusive yet omnipresent demon of the capital who tempts its inhabitants according to their characters and "infatuations." As Andrei Bely quipped, *"Chort 'Vecherov' stal chertoi"* ("the devil of the *Evenings* became a trait").[26]

The last of these stories from *Arabesques* is "The Diary of a Madman." The original title of the story was to have been "The Diary of a Mad Musician," and there is little doubt that it was conceived at first as a romantic *Kunstnovel* about a mad artist. This theme, embodied most successfully in Gogol's Piskaryov, the "victim of a frantic passion" in "Nevsky Prospect," was a theme Gogol found most attractive. He was enthusiastic about his friend Prince V. Odoevsky's[27] projected cycle *The House of Madmen* and knew the stories published separately that were to have been included in it: "Beethoven's Last Quartet" (1831, in an issue of *Northern Flowers*[28] that also contained an early sketch by Gogol under the influence of Walter Scott and the *école frénétique*), "Opere del Cavaliere Giambatista Piranesi" (1832), and "The Improvissatore" (1833). All three were tales of madmen obsessed with an *idée fixe* based on their art, the best example being Piranesi and his unrealizable architectural dreams. In his unfinished comedy "The Order of St. Vladimir of the Third Class," Gogol used the romantic theme of the *idée fixe* while downgrading it by making his hero a petty official whose obsession is the attainment of a particular medal (the appropriate surrogate in the case of a man whose "art" is that of bureaucracy). In the play the hero ends up being metamorphosed in his fantasy into the object of his desires: he imagines himself to be "The Order," in a typically Gogolian reversal of the categories of animate and inanimate.

The hero of "The Diary of a Madman" is also a civil servant obsessed with status. His madness is sparked, however, not by his lack of success in obtaining a medal but by the hopelessness of his love for the daughter of the Director of his department. Yet this love is based precisely on his obsession with rank. It is presented not as a spontaneous love prohibited by his low position in life; rather, the cause of his love is the "exalted" status of the object of his passion. Poprishchin's obsession with rank is hinted at from the very beginning of the story. He announces: "Yes, I confess, it it weren't for the respectability [*blagorodstvo*: the word suggests "nobility"] of the work, I "tragic" for his characters consists only in their loss of prestige or the blow to their pride caused by the strange events: the "soul" remains unaffected, since it does not exist or has already been lost.

Viktor Vinogradov has amply demonstrated Gogol's indebtedness to the "nosological" literature of the first quarter of the nineteenth century, where "cut-off, baked, suddenly disappearing and reappearing noses constantly flashed before the reader's eyes."[32] This craze was launched in Russian literature by the publication in 1804-1807 of the Russian translation of Lawrence Sterne's *The Life and Opinions of Tristram Shandy* ("Slawkenbergius's Tale" in Book IV is particularly relevant), where the nose is the subject of absurd debate, an object of envy or ridicule, and the basis for puns with veiled sexual reference. The many idioms and paronomastic set phrases of the Russian language which contain the word "nose"[33] were combined by Gogol with the literary traditions of "nosology" and served as the basis of the story's events. In fact, the central event could be described as a literal "realization" of a witticism by Pushkin using one such idiom: "And thus you surely will be 'with the nose' [i.e., "in hot water," "made a fool of"] when you find yourself without a nose."[34] (This epigram has a sexual connotation, namely that the nose's loss is due to venereal disease, and this is one of the "real" explanations of the event that Gogol plays on in the story through his hints about Kovalyov's amorous exploits). The primitive adventure novel with an exotic setting suitable for relating the adventures of cut-off noses or heads (Persia was a favorite place of action) provides the basic motif for the plot of the first part of "The Nose," the tale of the cut-off and baked nose (cf. "The Story of the Baked Head" in chapter XLV of James Morier's *The Adventures of Hajji Baba of Ispahan*), but the setting is shifted to everyday St. Petersburg and the central exotic event is treated quite naturalistically: Ivan Yakovlevich and his wife are less astounded by the fantastic nature of the event than they are afraid of its practical consequences. Gogol uses, as well, anecdotal material from the journalistic "miscellany" *(smes')* of the period for various subplots. Several articles had appeared in the journals during the twenties and early thirties about the new branch of medicine called "rhinoplastics" (plastic surgery on noses), which reported the facts of the medical procedure in a semi-humorous vein using nose puns. They are the source for the episode in which Kovalyov appeals to the "medic" for aid in "attaching" his nose, but Gogol comically negates the possibility of such an operation by the absurd reply of the doctor, who informs Kovalyov that the nose "can, of course, be attached; I could, probably, attach it right now for you; but I assure you that it would be worse for you." The mock "panegyrics" to the nose, another, strictly humorous, variant of journalistic "miscellanies" of the time involving noses, treated the nose as a personification of the virtues of a man and as a "sign of his honor": Kovalyov's reactions to the loss of his nose follow precisely such a rationale, and the energy with which he goes about attempting to retrieve his nose outdoes that of the most mortally offended romantic hero.

The grotesque nature of the story rests on the absurdity of the initial premise that a nose can belong simultaneously to the category of things and of animate beings. The first part of the story portrays it as a "cut-off" nose and ends with it being tossed into the Neva by the barber Ivan Yakovlevich. The second part relates the exploits of the nose, disguised in the uniform of a State Councillor, Kovalyov's unsuccessful efforts to pursue and retrieve it or at least seek justice (he appeals first to a newspaper office and only then to the police), the nose's capture, and finally Kovalyov's attempt to put it back (which is as unsuccessful as his earlier attempt in the Kazan Cathedral to put the "Nose" in his proper place). The illusion of a connection between these two parts of the story is created by the formal indication in each of them that the nose in question is precisely that of Major Kovalyov and by the parallelism of the beginning and ending of each part (awakening, horror, action; "all is shrouded in fog"). But no firm connection is ever established, nor is any explanation given of how the nose came to be in either of its estranged forms. Instead, the only episode in which it seems that the two plots will merge into one and the nose's disconcerting metamorphosis will finally be explained only intensifies the absurdity by piling on yet another irrelevant fact. The police officer who has apprehended the "Nose" just as he was about to escape to Riga with a false passport returns the "nose," neatly wrapped up in a rag in his pocket, to Kovalyov. His comment—that luckily he had his glasses on at the time of the capture and was thus able to tell that it was no "gentleman" but a "nose"—in no way accounts for the transformation that must have occurred for the "Nose" to be in his pocket.

The final resolution (Part III) is as inexplicable as the initial event: the nose reappears suddenly "in its proper place." Major Kovalyov is led out of the labyrinth which the author had constructed around him and goes on his merry, philistine way. We see the heroes of Part I and II, the barber and Kovalyov, together in the shaving scene in which neither mentions what has transpired. The story ends with the author, after confessing that there is "much that is improbable" in his narrative, justifying the "reality" of the absurd events he has detailed: ". . . and after all, where aren't there incongruities? . . ." The plane of the fantastic and the plane of the real are completely merged in this "extraordinarily strange" everyday tale.

"The Nose" thereby attacks not only the thematics, but the very form of the fantastic literature of late romanticism, in which the planes of the real and the supernatural were placed in graceful parallelism and the transition one to the other carefully, if ambiguously, motivated.[35] In Hoffmann's "The Sandman" or Pushkin's "The Queen of Spades" (1834), which Dostoevsky was later to call "the pinnacle of the art of the fantastic,"[36] the essence of the fantastic lies precisely in the hesitation between an interpretation of the events that rationally explains their apparently supernatural character and one conceding the existence of the supernatural. Dostoevsky writes in regard

xxii

to Pushkin's "The Queen of Spades": "You believe that Hermann really had a vision, and precisely in accordance with his world view, and yet at the end of the story, that is, having read it through, you don't know what to think. Did this vision emerge from the nature of Hermann, or is he really one of those who have come into contact with another world, [a world] of spirits evil and hostile to mankind? . . . Now this is art!"[37] The art Dostoevsky so admired was the author's ability to maintain the illusion of the impossible while offering sufficient motivation for its occurrence, in a way that forces the reader simultaneously to doubt and to believe in it.

Gogol's story is not a fantastic tale in essence, because of the absurd premise and the lack of hesitation between the real and the unreal. Although Gogol has his narrator or characters mention all the standard motifs used in the fantastic romantic short story to "explain the supernatural" (wine, rumor, dream, madness), he rejects them outright or plays with reversals of them. One such reversal is the catalogue of rumors that circulate about Kovalyov's story at the end of Part II. The usual function of rumors was to discredit the supernatural event (the rumors prove false or questionable) or to detail the real consequences of the character's folly after the event had proved a delusion; Gogol introduces rumors which themselves are called into doubt with particularly sharp irony. By debunking the rumors issuing from the fantastic event, he asserts the event's reality, which should have been more in question than the truth of rumors circulating in its wake. The total effect of the tale is not the hesitation between the real and the supernatural but the creation of a fictional universe terrifying in its detailed similarities to "vulgar," everyday reality yet impenetrable to the laws of common sense. Vinogradov catches much of the essence of the tale when he labels it a "naturalistic grotesque." "The Nose" contains in extreme form the essence of Gogol's later fiction, summarized by D.S. Mirsky in a few eloquent lines: "He made vulgarity reign where only the sublime and beautiful had reigned. This was *historically* the most important aspect of his work. Nor was the younger generation's general concept of him as a social satirist entirely unjustified. He did not paint (and scarcely knew) the social evils of Russia. But the caricatures he drew were, weirdly and terribly, *like* the reality around him; and the sheer vividness and convincingness of his paintings simply eclipsed the paler truth and irrevocably held the fascinated eye of the reader."[38]

"The Overcoat" is so thoroughly discussed in the articles by Eikhenbaum and Chizhevsky included here that it would be superfluous to treat the structure of the story or its place in Gogol's work in any more detail. It should be noted, however, that the story differs in many ways from *Dead Souls*, which was published the same year (1842). The *skaz* in *Dead Souls*, like that in "The Overcoat," has no consistent narrator. But the naturalistic presentation of "reality" is considerably heightened in *Dead Souls* by the careful delineation of the speech of the characters. The "verbal masks" that the characters wear are constructed in so convincing a manner and supported by so detailed a presentation of their gestures and environment that the reader fails to notice that they are just as much the narrator's "marionettes" as was Akaky Akakievich. In fact, hostile contemporary critics did not object to Gogol's treatment of his characters in *Dead Souls*, as they had in the case of Akaky Akakievich, but to his selection of such "low" types. (This was a continuation of Gogol's experiments in drama, e.g., *The Inspector General* [1836], where the illusion of the reality of characters was achieved by the convincingness of their spoken manner.)

The other respect in which the *skaz* in *Dead Souls* differs from that of "The Overcoat" is in its authorial digressions, which assume a consistency of theme and style that renders them a voice on a par with that of the characters. What results is a "verbal mosaic" of often antithetical elements. The main antithesis, that between the naturalistic descriptions and the sentimental "effusions" of the author, is intensified rather unsuccessfully in the chapters salvaged from the uncompleted Part II of *Dead Souls*. The increasingly moralistic tone of the author, couched in sentimental terms, was simply too grating against the background of the "low" themes and their naturalistic embodiment. In Part I of *Dead Souls*, the "verbal mosaic" held together because of Gogol's mastery in constructing various integral verbal masks (those of characters and narrator) in a polyphonic array; in Part II, it fell apart because of the predominance of one of those masks, that of the narrator-author's moralistic voice.

In Part II of *Dead Souls*, Gogol, whose entire work had been a polemic designed to undermine sentimentalism and romanticism, tried unsuccessfully to revive and reconcile sentimentalism with the naturalistic style, its "low" themes and characters, in whose name he had earlier rejected it. Dostoevsky, confronted by the heritage of Gogol's work as well as the extremes to which it had been taken by his imitators, succeeded in *Poor Folk* in accomplishing precisely what Gogol failed to do: a synthesis of naturalism and sentimentalism. The prevailing motivation in Gogol's case, his religious and moralistic orientation, had led to endless contradictions (cf. Tynyanov on the style of *Selected Passages from a Correspondence with Friends*, pp. 109 ff. below). Dostoevsky, for whom sentimentalism was merely a vehicle to transcend the limitations of crude naturalism, was able to combine naturalism and sentimentalism to achieve greater social and psychological depth, providing the foundations for the realistic prose of the second half of the century.

III

Dostoevsky led an isolated childhood, and early began to immerse himself in the world of fiction. His parents took him to see *The Robbers* when he was ten, as a result of which he conceived a passionate enthusiasm for Schiller. He read Derzhavin, Karamzin and Pushkin, and revelled in the novels of Walter Scott, which opened up a new exotic world to him. In "Petersburg Visions in Verse and Prose" (1861), Dostoevsky writes:

> . . . in my youthful fantasy I loved to imagine myself at times Pericles, or Caius Marius, or a Christian at the time of Nero, or a knight at the tournaments, or Edward Glendinning from Walter Scott's novel *The Monastery*, etc. etc. And what didn't I dream of in my youth. . . . There were no moments more full, holy and pure in my life. I was so lost in dreaming that I let my whole youth slip by me.[39]

Dostoevsky was intensely interested in literature, and his first works are predominantly concerned with literary reality. His early reading was mostly romantic, but around 1843 his tastes began to change, and while he was writing his first novel, *Poor Folk*, he was deeply impressed by Gogol's work. It was as a result of Gogol's vision of St. Petersburg which he found in "Nevsky Prospect" ("Everything is an illusion; everything is a dream") that Dostoevsky suddenly saw his surroundings with new eyes, as he later described in "Petersburg Visions":

> It seemed . . . that all this world, with all its inhabitants, both the strong and the weak, with all their habitations, whether beggars' shelters or gilded palaces, at this hour of twilight resembled a fantastic, enchanted vision, a dream which in its turn would instantly vanish and waste away as vapor into the dark blue heaven.[40]

Dostoevsky had come to perceive contemporary reality to be as fantastic as any romantic tale, and it is the task of his first stories to integrate the disparate literary world views of idealistic romanticism and Gogol's grotesque naturalism. The final result was what he called the "realism in a higher sense," the "fantastic realism" of his great novels.

The evolution that *Poor Folk* underwent in its three successive revisions from 1844 to April 1845, if Bem's hypothesis is correct,[41] contains in microcosm this movement away from romanticism towards naturalism. Dostoevsky started to write the novel in the typically romantic form of the confession of the young, wronged and helpless Varenka, possibly under the influence of Karamzin's sentimental tale *Poor Liza*, and only subsequently created the naturalist figure of Devushkin, whereupon the heroine's sentimental tale was restricted to Varenka's diary and assumed a secondary role. Similarly, in all of Dostoevsky's works written prior to his exile to Siberia in 1849, he performs a series of experiments in combining various elements of the sentimental and romantic traditions with naturalist themes and styles.

Dostoevsky's own evolution anticipated a turning point in the Natural School as a whole. The early physiological sketches which had provided the basis for the development of the Natural School were initially limited to the description of social groups, isolated by profession ("The Watercarrier," "The Organgrinders"), geographic location ("Petersburg Summits," "Moscow Markets"), or customs ("Weddings in Moscow," "Tea in Moscow"). The dominant focus was on the social milieu rather than on the individuals populating it.[42] Character was merely an adjunct of social type. But at the same time (around 1845), partly as a reaction against Gogol's epigones who had taken the comic short story to extremes of superficiality, and partly as a reaction against the limitations of "physiology," there was a reinfusion of sentimental elements which resulted in greater attention to the characters and less to their surroundings (see Vinogradov, p. 180 below). Using the later Gogolian model provided in "The Overcoat" and *Dead Souls*, and influenced by French philanthropic literature, the Natural School produced an offshoot called "sentimental naturalism" which attempted, often quite superficially, to inject notes of pathos into what remained essentially naturalist sketches. One group of writers, finding this view insufficient, called for a depiction of man based on his inner essence rather than on his external surroundings.[43] The leaders of this group, who belonged to the Petrashevsky circle, grounded their poetics in the philosophy of Utopian Socialism, and advocated the transformation of the physiological approach. Their literary-aesthetic principles were formulated in their most extreme form by Valerian Maikov, who, like the influential radical critic Belinsky, asserted that the role of belletristic literature was the popularization of socially important ideas. As opposed to Belinsky, however, Maikov and another member of the Petrashevsky circle, the poet Pleshcheev, advocated the examination of the depths of the soul in order to show how the social milieu formed and distorted human nature, in contradistinction to the "daguerrotype" sort of static depiction which gave no explanation of how the heroes became what they are. This approach followed from the utopian socialist principle of the innate goodness of man: in order to undo the damage wrought on the individual by society, one had to understand the mechanism at work.

> The sight of any sore is disgusting; but when you meet it not in the illustrations of a medical article . . . but on the body of a live person in whom you recognize your brother, a second self, —no matter what class he belongs to . . . —love will awaken in you, you will feel that sore on yourself, you will seize your own breast and feel with your own nerves that same pain which brings spasms to the limbs of your brother.[44]

It is utopian socialist ideology that motivates Dostoevsky's reinterpretation of Gogol. As a youth Dostoevsky had read the novels of George Sand

and Balzac which raised social questions, and the ideas of French Utopian Socialism were being discussed in the journals he read by the second half of the 1830s. His association with Belinsky, whom he met in May of 1845, when the critic read the manuscript of *Poor Folk* and acclaimed it as the first Russian social novel, reinforced Dostoevsky's literary concern with social questions. In his own words, he at first "passionately accepted all [Belinsky's] teachings."[45] But Belinsky's atheism quickly alienated Dostoevsky, who in 1847 became a member of the Petrashevsky circle, the members of which based their socialism on the ideal of Christian brotherhood. Like Fourier, Saint-Simon and Lamennais, they believed in a kind of religious humanism in which the highest values were man's right to equality and dignity. These ideals of the brotherhood of man are at the basis of Dostoevsky's tales about the poor clerk.

Another contributing factor to Dostoevsky's rethinking of naturalist poetics was Hoffmann's work. During the craze of Russian Hoffmannism in the 1820s, which continued into the 1830s,[46] Hoffmann's influence was primarily thematic and formal. Dostoevsky returns, however, to the psychological dimension of the fantastic in Hoffmann, which had been previously explored by Pushkin in "The Queen of Spades." Dostoevsky had read all of Hoffmann in German and/or Russian by the time he was seventeen, and in his early period, particularly in *The Double* and *The Landlady*, reinterprets Gogol's treatment (whether serious, as in "A Terrible Vengeance," or parodic, as in "The Nose") of romantic themes using Hoffmann's psychologism. Like Hoffmann, Dostoevsky makes use of the fantastic within a realistic setting, and achieves grotesque effects by the juxtaposition of the extraordinary to the everyday. But in Hoffmann's Berlin stories the fantastic takes the form of events whose reality is ambiguous, accepted by some characters whose sanity is in question and rejected by others who take a "practical" view. The author reserves judgment and leaves the reader vacillating on the borderline between reality and fantasy. For Dostoevsky, however, the fantastic results from the refraction of reality through the abnormal consciousness of the hero. The grotesque in Dostoevsky is a product of the tension between the external world as seen through another's eyes and the inner reality of the hero's consciousness.[47] And to emphasize the inherent disparity between these two views, Dostoevsky portrays abnormal consciousnesses which are distorted either by physical disease (delirium is the source of the unconscious in its purest state, as in "Mr. Prokharchin," *The Landlady*, and later, *Crime and Punishment*), or by mental disorders. The heroes in *The Double* and "A Faint Heart" go insane, while Devushkin and the dreamer in *White Nights* simply have distorted views of the world, the result of injured pride (Devushkin) or bookish isolation (the Dreamer).

Dostoevsky's first three works, *Poor Folk, The Double*, and "Mr. Prokharchin" (all published in 1846), take the naturalist theme of the petty clerk and reinterpret it, using sentimental and romantic elements to add the moral and psychological dimensions Dostoevsky found contained in Utopian Socialism and in Hoffmann's work. *Poor Folk* uses the sentimental form of the correspondence between two lovers, *The Double* combines the mock heroic epic (via Gogol's "Two Ivans" and *Dead Souls*) with the German romantics' favorite theme of the double and attendant madness, and "Mr. Prokharchin" also uses a romantic theme, that of the miser whose "bedscreens are the walls of his castle" while his treasure chest stands "deep below" (under his bed).[48] In each case the implicit juxtaposition to the earlier tradition is used to motivate the naturalist thematics, and the embodiment of these thematics Dostoevsky finds in Gogol's work.

The choice of Gogol is of course an obvious one, as he dominated literature at the time Dostoevsky was forming his style, but there are more specific reasons as well. Gogol had taken the theme of the petty clerk, which had become a mere comic convention, and made it into a moral allegory by the reinfusion of sentimental elements. In the process, he touched on a set of motifs central to Dostoevsky's thoughts about the clerk's psychology, as in "Diary of a Madman." Dostoevsky rejects the taxonomic and comic treatments of Petersburg "low life" to return to Gogol and extract what Dostoevsky saw as the essence of his predecessor's writing.

Dostoevsky replaces Gogol's religious morality with the ideology of Utopian Socialism. Gogol pits his poor clerk against representatives of power who assume allegorical status—The Important Personage, The General; Dostoevsky presents the clerk's social milieu less allegorically by surrounding his heroes with an array of secondary characters—Pokrovsky, Gorshkov—whose similar fates serve to generalize the hero's experience.[49] As Valerian Maikov put it, "For [Gogol] the individual is important as a representative of a given society or circle; for [Dostoevsky] the society itself is interesting for its influence on the personality of the individual."[50] Gogol had applied motifs used in the high genre of German romanticism, "imposture," schizophrenia and ambition, to the figure of the "little man." But Gogol characteristically renders animate objects inanimate: his use of metonymy transforms people into mere appendages of their clothing, facial features, or names, using grotesque verbal masks to obliterate human personality. Dostoevsky also wanted to rework the same romantic motifs using the poor clerk. Repelled by Gogol's depersonalization of his heroes, who were typically inarticulate, Dostoevsky had his characters reveal themselves through their verbal manner. Thus while it is possible to say that Dostoesky was "correcting" Gogol by humanizing his heroes, it is also true that Dostoevsky saw himself as continuing Gogol's attempts at adding greater depth to the comic convention of the poor clerk.

Central to Dostoevsky's interpretation of the utopian socialist ideal of the integrity of the individual is the concept of pride, which is the motivating